D1525503

A Feeling of History

Peter Zumthor

Mari Lending

A Feeling of History

With a series of photographs by
Hélène Binet

Scheidegger & Spiess

"I confess I do not believe in time.
I like to fold my magic carpet, after use,
in such a way as to superimpose
one part of the pattern upon another.
Let visitors trip. And the highest enjoyment
of timelessness—in a landscape
selected at random—is when I stand
among rare butterflies and their food plants.
This is ecstasy, and behind the ecstasy
is something else, which is hard to explain.
It is like a momentary vacuum into
which rushes all that I love. A sense of
oneness with sun and stone."

Vladimir Nabokov
Speak, Memory (1966)[1]

Preamble
Mari Lending

Modernity and mining can be summed up in many
disparate words: industrialization, modernization,
exploitation, wealth and poverty, life and death, local
rupture and global flow, backwardness and industrial triumph, nature as a resource to be technologized
or aestheticized, all the way from the picturesque
to the technologically sublime.

Mining in the nineteenth century, however, was
also a locus of love. "Crystallization," Stendhal's
illustrious metaphor for love, was conceived in situ at
the salt mines of Hallein near Salzburg. Stendhal
referred to the local custom—still practiced today—
of throwing bare branches into the depths of the
abandoned mines. When pulled back into the light
months later, the branches were covered with
sparkling salt crystals. This diamond-like filigree led
Stendhal to a sophisticated theory of the stages
of love, as presented in his 1822 treatise *De l'amour*

(Love): (1) Admiration; (2) "You think, 'How delightful it would be to kiss her, to be kissed by her,' and so on ..."; (3) Hope; (4) Love is born; (5) The first crystallization begins; (6) Doubt creeps in; (7) The second crystallization.[2]

The point is that love changes reality. The metamorphosis is an intervention as well as a phenomenon in the eye of the beholder—perfecting, framing, interpreting, and reinventing what is naturally and culturally given. Initially obscure, the treatise's first edition reached only a few readers, but Stendhal later reworked the material into the romantic short story "Le rameau de Salzbourg" (The Salzburg Bough).[3] Here, he elaborated his theory of crystallization in the form of a lovely piece of fiction that was included as an appendix in the posthumously published 1853 edition. Soon *De l'amour* became a classic.

The constellation of kissing and mining, love and chemistry, sudden death and promises of eternity appears to be a topos in modern fiction. Yet, in what Franz Kafka deemed the most wonderful story in the world—Johann Peter Hebel's 1811 "Unverhofftes Wiedersehen" (The Unexpected Reunion)—it is not so much the sad love story as the breathtaking temporalities unfolding that make the most memorable impression. Early one morning a young miner kisses his bride-to-be before leaving for work in his black miner's suit ("a miner is always dressed ready for his own funeral"), and the same day the miner meets his foreshadowed fate. After the woman has spent more than fifty years in quiet mourning, the beloved's body is recovered from deep down in a mine shaft, perfectly preserved in ferrous vitriol, untouched by decay and as beautiful as the day he died. Thus the lovers—the male sleeping beauty and the old lady—are reunited, a convergence that introduces a twisted temporality into this story of faithful, if unfulfilled, love. Hebel's awe-inspiring marking of the passage of time from the sudden death to the temporally distorted reunion takes up a substantial portion of this (very short) short story and deserves to be quoted in its entirety:

"In the meantime the city of Lisbon in Portugal was destroyed by earthquake, the Seven Years' War came and went, the Emperor Francis I died, the Jesuits were dissolved, Poland was partitioned, the Empress Maria Theresa died, and Struensee was executed, and America became independent, and the combined French and Spanish force failed to take Gibraltar. The Turks cooped up General Stein in the Veterane Cave in Hungary, and the Emperor Joseph died too. King Gustavus of Sweden conquered Russian Finland, the French Revolution came and the long war began, and the Emperor Leopold II too was buried. Napoleon defeated Prussia, the English bombarded Copenhagen, and the farmers sowed and reaped."[4]

Hebel's little piece of fiction thus brings us to 1809, when the body resurfaces from the rubble and the vitriol. One can only imagine how Stendhal, himself a master of literary ellipses and an astute eyewitness to world-changing political events, would have admired (and maybe he did) this sublime list of world-historical events infused into a local love story played out against the backdrop of the Swedish mines of Falun.

Stendhal's intricate theory of crystallization, on the one hand, and Hebel's conflation of distorted temporalities and a hyperbolic world-historical panorama on the other, spring to mind in relation to Peter Zumthor's architectural interventions at the abandoned nineteenth-century zinc mines at Allmannajuvet, close to Sauda on the west coast of Norway. In Stendhal, the chemical process crystallizes dissolved minerals, transforming a natural *objet trouvé* into pure beauty. The time involved in the metamorphosis from nature to culture and the emphasis on the subjective experience of aesthetic, sensual phenomena are evoked in different ways by the four structures that are now installed in the dramatic terrain along the old mining trail. Hebel's exposition of warped temporalities—the synchronizing of something personal, subjective, and out of sync within a factual, chronological framework—and the weaving of a local history into a world-historical fabric reverberate in the ways in which the new pavilions frame and evoke the invisible history of the place. Discoursing on love, both Stendhal and Hebel address profound questions of history, time, and temporalities in ways that bear comparison with the effects of Zumthor's contemporary elaboration of both the landscape and the cultural-industrial vestiges of the mines at Allmannajuvet.

Mari Lending   Having seen the Allmannajuvet Zinc Mine Museum project when you first presented it in Sauda in 2004, and now on its completion in 2016, I'm struck by how these pavilions tie in with a distinct awareness of history and time that saturates your architectural production.

Peter Zumthor   Looking back, I see that my work and my specific approach to architecture has developed over a long period of time since I received my first modernistic training at the Kunstgewerbe-schule Basel, modeled on Bauhaus ideas. Then, design was all about being innovative, about finding new solutions to mostly old problems, about fighting history, even overcoming history. Since then, my approach to design and history has changed a lot. Looking at the world around me now makes me realize: Everything I see is history. Almost everything that surrounds us, our landscapes, villages, and cities, down to our houses and the rooms where we live, is full of history; we just have to see it. Everything has been made by someone, by people I don't know, people I have never met, and most of them long dead. Increasingly, that is a reassuring feeling, it makes me feel part of the world.

   I like to think that, with my work, I add a little bit to all of these things that are already here, in the world.

I would like the buildings I make to say: "I understand something about what is around me." I don't want them to give the impression of being aliens, of having nothing to do with what is already there. This is not an aesthetic matter, at least not primarily; it does not start with having to establish formal contact with the surroundings. It is like searching for a kind of sameness in the form of emotional contact—an emotional reaction to the surroundings, expressed through architecture.

Johann Peter Hebel also wrote a poem about Basel in the local dialect: "Z'Basel an mym Rhy" (In Basel on My Rhine). This was set to music and in my youth it was a popular song in praise of the city. Hebel has become part of my memories of Basel. I hear his song and I immediately feel what Basel smells like on a Saturday morning, when the shops are about to open. So when I'm in a new city, I can go out on a Saturday morning, walk the streets, and feel at home, right away. It's a bit like Nabokov and the butterflies. It gives me a strong feeling of place, of presence and belonging. This feeling of history is different from the factual history conserved on paper and taught at universities. That is a kind of "history-history," an intellectual system that works from document to document, from paper to paper; ten papers become 100 papers, and so on.

For me, this has little to do with the real things I experience on a site or in a landscape. As an architect, I am interested in the history that is stored and accumulated in landscapes, places, and things. The things I can see and feel in the landscape are physical and real, no matter how mute, hidden, and mysterious they might at first appear.

ML   This way of talking about actual and factual history resembles Josef Albers's distinction between factual and actual facts, which was so crucial to his perceptual aesthetics. In his 1963 *Interaction of Color* he defined the factual as that which is "not undergoing changes," while the actual "is something not fixed, but changing with time."[5] History was not of much interest to Albers. Your way of distinguishing actual from factual history rather makes me think of Stendhal, who when arriving in Pompeii felt "transporté dans l'antiquité" ("transported back to Antiquity").[6] Face-to-face with Antiquity, experiencing the ruins and the rubble firsthand, "one immedi- ately knows more than a scholar," he mused, describing the thrilling pleasures of experiential immediacy. Yet places like Pompeii—destroyed, restored, recon- structed, styled, and reinvented over and over throughout history, not least in modern times—can make it hard to believe in any kind of immediacy

beyond the ever-changing present that de facto constitutes the history of monuments. For Stendhal, the historical site itself induced a feeling of time travel, and the place revealed a feeling of history of a different sort—a sort that he found far more profound than scholarly history. Through experience, the history of the place came alive, so to speak.

PZ   What you say about Stendhal fascinates me. I like to look at a place, feel it, understand it, and then the form I'm looking for starts to emerge in an intuitive process. I want to create buildings that speak about the time of their place and talk to people. So I have to do something to make memory speak. Art can do that: the art of building, just as much as writing, painting, or music. When listening to a piece of music or walking in a beech wood forest in summer, something touches me, something that I seem to have experienced before. And now I experience it again in the new context of a particular moment, and then old and new sensations intermingle and the brain tries to understand. In these moments I'm looking for new intensities, I think. So when a piece of art or architecture makes memory speak to you, as Nabokov says, it is mingled with the world or whatever you know, maybe conflating the actual and the factual. Memory is now, a kind of happening at this very moment.

ML   Memory and history are not the same,
yet they might merge on a personal level. When you,
through architecture, try to make memory speak,
you are dealing with memories and histories that are
not your own, and with histories that might also
have been forgotten by the locals at the many places
around the world where you are building.

PZ   Landscapes and places store memories, they
save traces of lives long gone. What fascinates me
about these traces is that they are real, they are
unique, they are always authentic. To me, landscapes
are historical documents; I can try to read and
interpret the place where I have to act as an architect.
With my design I can help create an awareness;
like a magnifying glass, it can help me look closely at
a place, discover remnants of human activities that
are easily overlooked but clearly there. At Sauda,
I was fascinated by the marks a small group of people
left behind on the barren Allmannajuvet ravine,
traces of their hard labor at the zinc mine that was
in operation there from 1883 to 1899. Looking at
those traces, I started to feel respect for the work they
did and the lives they must have lived. I wanted to
make visitors aware of that.

        I want my buildings to be connected to the history
of a place. That's important to me. What has long

been mute starts to speak, sparks appear, emotions rise to the surface and we start to understand. It's like Hebel's story about the miner; there is the larger history of international industry, markets, and the exploitation of the working class, and there is the local history of the place of my intervention, which in turn, if I do my work well, might speak about the whole.

ML   In your writings and lectures you often talk about architecture through other art forms, particularly literature and music. Or maybe that is the wrong way to phrase it, as you are in fact talking about art in its own right, and not just as a means of explaining something about architecture. In any case, the architect of one of my favorite buildings said something that you might agree with, namely, that the "best architect always uses the fewest materials." Something amazing happened in the material constellation of cast concrete and plaster casts when, at Yale University in 1963, Paul Rudolph reinstalled two hundred Assyrian, Egyptian, Hellenistic, Greek, Roman, and medieval casts through the nine floors and thirty-seven levels of the Art & Architecture Building. Josef Albers himself had exiled the enormous collection from the school's former building on his arrival in New Haven in 1950. Synonymous with Beaux-Arts training, the casts were anathema to a Bauhaus teacher like Albers.

Rudolph, however, who accidentally came across the survivors of Albers's iconoclasm, distributed these *objets trouvés* throughout the complex spatiality of his new building, creating unexpected vistas, sensual surprises, bodily experiences. The salvaged pieces are fragments that mutely point to lost contexts, world-views, and systems of meaning—objects that physically merge history and setting, as Walter Benjamin might have put it. In a discreet and surprising way, Rudolph integrated these fragile, incredibly untimely ruins into his poetic, Brutalist structure. The result is strikingly emotional and profoundly historical.

Rudolph continually reiterated his view that architecture is a highly emotional affair—and more so than the other arts, including painting and music: "Architecture obviously deals with a lot of things, including a lot of mundane aspects, but the final result is highly, highly emotional."[7] He succeeded in demonstrating that memory is an actual event when he reintroduced these homeless and devalued remnants. Needless to say, there's a considerable distance between a 1960s concrete structure populated with nineteenth-century relics in New Haven and the remains of the mining enterprise that you've been dealing with at Allmanna-juvet. Still, there appear to be some similarities, not least in effect, in how discarded or overlooked remnants of the past might take on a new significance in radically recharged contexts—contexts that perhaps only architecture can create.

PZ   I saw Paul Rudolph's Yale Art & Architecture Building in New Haven in the late 1960s but have no specific memory of the plaster casts that he integrated into the design. With my modernistic background, I was probably conditioned to overlook them at the time. Today, having grown a bit older, I see his building differently, and his approach makes a lot of sense to me. I think it is important to include traces of the past, to weave them into a new building, integrating them, overlaying, or absorbing them. The palimpsest is a nice metaphor for this kind of architectural layering on historical ground. Paraphrasing Jenny Holzer, I would say: "Integrate things from before any time you have the chance." This gives me the chance to lend my building greater depth. I could, of course, design architecture that stimulates memories of the past through formal and material allusions to history, but I think nothing is more powerful than the historical substance itself.

Clearly, there are many ways of evoking a feeling of history and the layers of history that are embedded in places. When I worked in Berlin for ten years on a building to mark the former Gestapo headquarters, I kept hoping that the historians there would understand that the history of a place is also stored in physical things—remnants, even rubble—that help us to understand it in a way that goes beyond scientific texts and didactic explanations. Maybe not beyond, but it is a different mode of understanding, based on emotions rather than intellect. This was the moment in my career when I first started to understand that apart from academic learning, there is such a thing as emotional learning. My understanding of it was triggered by the historians and curators of the Topography of Terror Foundation, who did not want the building to speak to the place. The topography of the site had a significance of its own, having been a place of terror and the actual place where Nazi terror was conceived. I think the curators of the Foundation didn't want the building to stimulate emotions in its response to the site and its subject matter. "You are dramatizing history," they told me. But actually what I wanted was to let the terrain speak for itself and have the historical interpretation and didactics on the upper floors of the new building. My aim was to give visitors a chance to experience the place first, to get a sense of the place where everything happened, to see what had happened to the historic ground since then, and to experience on their own what is happening to it now.

Some time ago I read an interview with the Swiss writer Thomas Hürlimann in which he says that our

personal memory lives from images, not from facts. Often, what we see will evoke images in our minds that are associated with memories. I believe that might be what Stendhal felt when he saw the ruins of Pompeii. And it works the other way round, too. The images that we remember are inevitably related to feelings and emotions. Abstract facts are secondary. This is the starting point for most of my projects, such as the Shelter for Roman Archaeological Ruins in Chur, the Kolumba Art Museum in Cologne, and certainly my two Norwegian projects: the Steilneset Memorial in Vardø and the Mining Museum in Sauda. They are all specifically about history as stored in landscapes, places, and things, about memories and the emotions associated with them. However, in retrospect, I realize that memories and emotions evoked by the places I have to build on are the starting point for practically all of my projects—not just the ones that explicitly deal with historic monuments.

ML   Your work—the buildings as well as the books— has often been phenomenologically framed and interpreted by critics, for obvious reasons. You have repeatedly written and talked about memory, experience, and place. Still, the importance of such qualities resonates with architectural ideas and forms handed down from ancient Rome—or earlier—

through Renaissance treatises, and beyond. Somehow the idea of history being stored in landscapes, places, and things, and your concern with emotions and memory recall the classical, rhetorical tradition's emphasis on physical gestures, as manifested also in architecture, and the idea of a common ground for shared convictions and experiences. Remember, the idea that gestures were seen to be closer to emotions than words resulted in the exhibition of the murdered Cicero's hands, and not only his head, at the Forum Romanum. The belief that architectural form might externalize thought, that buildings can give shape to feelings and history, and not least the idea that architecture can make dead matter appear alive, excite emotion, memory, and associations in the beholder, and even make the absent present or the invisible visible—these are all traits that appear to be fundamental to your architectural ethos.

History gives life to recollection, wrote Cicero in *De oratore,* while Alberti and other Renaissance Humanists entrusted to art and architecture the task of keeping alive the memory of humanity. I find that your work, the built and the written, evokes these traditions in European philosophy, aesthetics, and architecture, and that the phenomenological framing might be a bit myopic.

PZ Well, my method might be called phenomeno-logical—before I understand, I have to look and wonder—but my deepest interest is to feel the time of my places through looking. But then, as an architect, can I really give shape to feelings and history? As I see it, you can stir a feeling for history or bygone times, but feelings have no shape. I certainly agree with the idea that architecture can make dead matter appear alive and excite emotion, but to make something absent present is, of course, a contra-diction in itself.

ML Still, in Sauda what you had in hand at the beginning was just a landscape, as mute or as eloquent as its wider environment. Allmannajuvet is not really the kind of sublime landscape that made the Norwegian west coast iconically famous in the nineteenth century. Here, neither the sublime nor the beautiful comes for free, whether one approaches from the east over the—admittedly beautiful—medieval route through the mountains or from the west from the coast.

The mine and mining culture are long gone. By intervening architecturally at this particular site, basically one curve among many that might easily be passed unheedingly, you are invoking something that would otherwise be incomprehensible, illegible,

invisible, lost, forgotten. You do something with architectural means that makes an obsolete reality present again.

PZ   I believe it is more about creating a feeling for the things that are absent than about creating a feeling of presence for things lost. So I try to stimulate a feeling for things that are no longer here or for the lost context of things that are still here. Both in Cologne's Kolumba and in Sauda—in fact, in most of my buildings—you might be struck by a slight air of melancholy. You are reminded of a feeling for some-thing that is not there, but which you seem to know well. You visit the Kolumba Art Museum in Cologne, and before long you see that this was once a Gothic church built on top of a Romanesque church, and then you see some Roman walls, and as you look the excavations get to you and make you wonder what it must have been like. I love the idea that a new work of architecture can be a gesture that inspires inter-est and respect. Architectural gestures may say more than words, or at least something different than words. The physical gestures of a building are more primal, more directly connected to the sensory capac-ities of our bodies than to thoughts and words. You say Alberti wanted to keep the memory of humanity alive through art and architecture, and that

touches on the essence of architecture in a way. It is always and only now, in the moment, that architecture can create a feeling for history and the absent. Everything happens in the present. So, as Nabokov says, there's no point in believing in time.

ML   Nabokov longed for ecstatic timelessness, even for what he calls a momentary vacuum, a state outside time, some kind of eternal presence of sun, stone, and his beloved butterflies. How do you understand this constellation of timelessness and presence, and how may it translate architecturally?

PZ   Nabokov makes it clear that his passion and compassion for memories always happen in the present and only in the present, and that his happiest moments are right now, right here, perfectly captured in the presence of butterflies. I've said it before and I say it again because it is so important to me: I want my architecture to be linked to layers of life and time; I want to understand why and how a particular object might set in motion a particular strain of emotions and memories. And architecture is about history precisely then when it ties in with the world of the here and now. Places and buildings are real, they are concrete, they are here.

ML   Being a historian and not an architect, I find your dichotomy between scholarly history and the history of buildings—or what is stored in buildings, landscapes, and things—slightly troubling. Personally, I find paper, and even dusty archives, auratic. The pleasure that in happy moments I find in piles of old documents is incredibly real, emotional; it's yet another source for the "Speak, Memory" figure, crystallizing from paper, paper, paper … Yet the one thing does not necessarily eclipse the other. For example, I have never read a description of the Battle of Waterloo that felt more real, and unforgettable in its portrayal of the absurd chaos and stupidity of war than the one Stendhal presents in the novel *La Chartreuse de Parme* (The Charterhouse of Parma), bordering, emblematically, on the actual and the factual. Art, including architecture, can of course document, explain, and portray moments of the past differently from what you call history-history; but paper and historiography are also an inexhaustible source of pleasure when we try to understand fragments of the past.

PZ   That you are so animated by the emotional power of those archives makes me smile. I love the way you talk about them. I am, of course, biased by my experiences with historians and art historians who haven't a clue about emotions as a part of our cultural understanding. As I already mentioned, in my Berlin project I witnessed historians getting irritated and even annoyed by the notion that architecture could help explain the territories that they are researching, writing and talking about. That was a bad experience; needless to say, there are also great thinkers and scholars who have inspired me immensely; so of course, right there, the dichotomy collapses.

In my projects in Sauda and Vardø, for instance, I found great partners who understood my approach to history. The historian Liv Helene Willumsen wrote abstracts of the biographies of the "witches" burned at the stake at Steilneset, Vardø.[8] They are factual, but at the same time so well written and composed that they have the quality of concrete poetry evoking a very specific emotional understanding, empathy, and compassion. We printed them on pieces of silk which are now hanging on the walls inside the building. Reading those texts for the first time brought tears to my eyes. When you read what absurd things the victims were accused of at the beginning and how after some time they confessed to having practiced all of them, you can imagine very well what happened in between without anybody telling you.

I often tell my young collaborators in the atelier to be emotional, to trust their intuition, not to rationalize

and start explaining too early in the process. They might kill their design intuitions by rationalizing. There is often an inflated layer of talking and arguing that is more disruptive than useful in trying to find the right architecture for a given task and site. Thinking is vital, of course, but to me thinking is a line, while emotions and intuitions enable us to penetrate much deeper, biographical spaces. So when designing, I look for deeper reactions and intuitions that have not yet been put into words or have not yet evoked a physical form. To me, the basic emotions of designing a building and experiencing the real building much later are the same.

ML You talk about history and a feeling of history, but it strikes me that you are really talking about time and temporalities. In fact, you somehow remind me of the art historian George Kubler. Appalled by what he termed the "bristling ugliness" of the concept of "material culture," Kubler, in his 1962 *The Shape of Time,* invented a "History of Things." This history of things is not about chronological development and the ordering of objects and events in the conventional sense. Kubler launched a history of things in an attempt to "reunite ideas and objects under the rubric of visual form," as he put it, including "both artifacts and works of art, both replicas and unique examples, both tools and expression—in short, all materials worked by human hands under the guidance of connected ideas developed in temporal sequence [...] From all these things a shape in time emerges," as Kubler wonderfully sums it up.[9] If we add landscape to this, it comes quite close to describing something critical at work in your architecture. The notion of things as part of time strikes me as a better approximation of how you en-vision architecture's relationship to history and their conflation, or perhaps coexisting temporalities, in certain landscapes, objects, or buildings.

PZ I just discovered Kubler, thanks to you. His thoughts are a revelation to me. His "shape of time" formula is inspiring. I love the idea that time has a shape and we just have to learn to see it. With this image in mind, I can look deep into time and feel connected. I can see the things that Kubler called "primary objects"—recurring formal solutions to identical problems and the creation of artifacts. For a moment I feel as if I could transcend factual history and become part of the larger context of human existence. First, I feel a timeline and I'm at the end of this line—in an uncomfortable position in a way. But then, I see so many things—things from the past—and I'm part of it all, so much so that the feeling of time as a line dissolves; it's all one, all presence. Nabokov again.

It makes me wonder if there are building types in architecture like the primary objects Kubler talks about. Pondering these questions in relation to my work fires my imagination. Yes, I want to answer my briefs with the strength of primary building types, because I think they really do exist and might speak of ancient traditions we don't really know anymore.

Kubler's notion of primary objects has also enlarged my range of emotional perception. When I look at some of the wonderful pieces in the collection of the Los Angeles County Museum of Art, for instance, or when I read Neil MacGregor's book *A History of the World in 100 Objects,*[10] I'm made powerfully aware that emotion has a shape. More than explaining his objects, MacGregor seems to describe why he loves them and I share his feelings right away. And it's funny, having grown up with modernistic principles, I should be disturbed by the fact that I'm reacting to a book, to words, to mere photographs, rather than originals. It's fascinating, and moving, to realize how MacGregor makes me see the artifacts. They come alive and I haven't even seen them! Now I want to see them.

ML   At Allmannajuvet, there is surely nothing even close to a strong or primary object in sight. So now the

pavilions perform the history of the place; the ensemble of small structures somehow resurrects fragments of the past by architectural means. Are you also reinventing or reenacting what is irretrievably lost as part of a program that also aspires to serve as a museum?

PZ   Yes, I am. I used physical fragments of the past— almost forgotten and easily overlooked—to create a new project that looks at the history of the place. I started by looking, by trying to understand the modest traces left in the landscape. Very slowly, I began to see the big picture. I discovered the mining trail. I saw where the water was channeled to be brought down to the washery. I saw where the rocks and cliffs had been cut into the canyon. We took the historic mining trail as a guideline for the visitors' tour of the site. Now when you walk along it from building to build- ing—that's when you start discovering. The new path on the forgotten trail acts as a tie-in to the past in the form of movement and moments. Installed in the landscape like pearls on a chain, the new singu- lar buildings follow the trail, marking scarce and extremely modest traces of the former mine, whose operations were closely related to great poverty. The director's stately residence down in the town of Sauda still exists.

I'm happy that through our project the work of the miners and their poor working conditions in the harsh landscape of the canyon are also now being commemorated.

But in terms of architectural form, we are replicating nothing, nothing at all. The new structures are different from the ones that were once part of the mining enterprise. They are contemporary objects, employing scaffolding not unlike that used in Vardø. The wooden constructions are precisely engineered to meet the structural needs of the black boxes sitting in wooden cages. The scaffolding is untreated, unworked, kept as simple as possible. The black volumes have an industrial look. Together they create a specific presence in the canyon landscape and speak of its history. And once more, you can see the amazing effect that architecture can have when it marks a place. You start to see the landscape around the buildings in a new way: The buildings introduce scale, the landscape and the topography start to speak; they become bigger, and at the same time you start to focus.

In addition, from the very beginning I considered it vital to relate the road-stop project not only to the history of the place, but also to contemporary life in Sauda. So the mining café not only serves tourists; it can also accommodate local events. The space is therefore heated for use in winter when there are

no tourists and the interior of the café is designed
to offer an intensified view of the impressive landscape
of the canyon. The view is framed and the moment
you sit down at a table, you experience the panoramic
effect. The black box emphasizes the colors of the
landscape, and at the same time you seem to be
inside a looking glass, a close-up, almost face to face
with the cliffs and the trees. Perhaps you will find
yourself looking not just *at* the place, but deeper *into*
it; you might even snap out of the tourist mode
and actually start to see.

ML   I know that Hebel's "Unexpected Reunion,"
one of many tales on the miner of Falun, is among your
favorites, and it is not hard to understand why.
Here, the great narratives and linear time are caught
in the ellipsis; or in fact, it is a kind of elliptical anti-
ellipsis, so to speak—the bracketing of the epic sweep
of history between cruelly sundered personal histories. Either way, the list of chronologically ordered
historical events testifies to the passing of time on
a grand scale. This inventory of factual, world-historical
political incidents is dramatically juxtaposed with
lived history and the singular, private moment captured
in the kiss—a kiss that anticipates death, but also
the future. This kiss encapsulates its own actual contemporaneity as well as constituting a new potential

future contemporaneity occurring half a century later: two contemporary moments that are not governed by linear time. The kiss has a time of its own, preserving the singular moment and pointing toward experiences unfolding in alternative and competing temporalities, beyond mere chronology.

Somebody who dies young remains young, and may be remembered as unmarked by time and decay. But Hebel adds yet another layer to this process of recollection. The twisted temporalities have a very material basis, as the body is protected and embalmed by minerals. The young lover is perfectly preserved by the mine itself. Conventionally, such a preservation of beauty and such a distortion of time have to be explained philosophically or described metaphorically. Here, however, it is factual, material, and physical. It is a product of the mine.

PZ   The story is wonderfully complex in its layout of past and present. It is important to remember that Hebel, a priest, was also the editor of the *Kalendergeschichten* (Calendar Stories), in which "Unexpected Reunion" was published. This almanac was a kind of predecessor to modern newspapers. People in the countryside used to subscribe to it at a time when they had hardly any books and little news from the outside world. Hebel's stories were a weave of contemporary news and small pieces of fiction, a grand project of enlightenment on a local scale. The intention was didactic, but the writing had, and still has, a beauty and a serenity that make the stories deeply touching. The tale of the miner and his fiancée has so many layers. It is obviously about love. But then all of a sudden Hebel pulls his readers up short with temporalities that come very close to a miracle, despite the perfectly natural explanation. For a moment time comes to a halt; for a moment my knowledge of the past is suspended. What is gone is gone, we usually say, but here something thought to be irrevocably lost comes back with almost painful beauty. In architecture I cannot create anything as cogent as that, but I would like to get close. What I have learned from Hebel's story of the miner and his fiancée is that I have to strike a special chord to make memory speak.

ML   You have described Allmannajuvet as an open-air museum. Yet somehow, it is the opposite, at least according to conventional definitions, particularly in the Nordic world, where open-air museums have a long tradition of decontextualizing, constructing, and displaying the vernacular within larger schemes, representing the nation or the region topo-mimetically or otherwise. You obviously think differently about the open-air museum.

PZ   Allmannajuvet might be called an in-situ open-air museum that works with authentic remnants. There is an archeological approach to it. The little traces, the mining trails, are actually a concrete fact in the landscape. They are actual, existing lines. As such, they are already a kind of open-air museum in their own right, so that the architectural work is about sensing the history of the place and trying to make things visible in a way that allows people to respond to them emotionally, rather than passively "learning" about the site. The new buildings are designed to be part of a larger whole; they are placed next to the remains of the foundations of the old buildings and mining installations. Thus, for example, the new museum building clings to the rocks at the exact same place where ore was once dropped down into the canyon to be washed, before being shipped off to England. The path from the national tourist road up to the former mining trail consists of stairs hewn into the natural rock by local stone masons. It's a completely contemporary masterpiece of craftsmanship that intensifies the topography and the act of moving your body up to the old mining path, from one world into another.

But it is also a museum in a more traditional sense. The gallery shows objects found in the mine, such as buckets, cubes of dynamite, and mining tools. The

display is reminiscent of a nineteenth-century museum with small glass showcases—a kind local history museum in situ. The objects are illuminated by the daylight that trickles into the black boxes through narrow light shafts from above. It is the same light that once fell on this modest mining equipment. In addition, we commissioned four books. These are originals which exist only on site. They give an abstract picture of the mining operation, of its history and geology. Kjartan Fløgstad, the Norwegian writer originally from Sauda, made an anthology, *Sub Terra, Sub Sole,* compiling mining in fiction across different times and languages. Of course, I made sure that the collection contains Hebel's "Unexpected Reunion." There is also a book that presents the architectural project as it developed over the years, as well as a survey of the local vegetation. But rather than being rational or scientific, the whole project is aimed at our capacities for emotional learning. The architecture avoids grand gestures and works with contemporary industrial simplicity. Just as Johann Peter Hebel's story reaches back into the past and acquires a powerful presence, so I'm trying to stimulate a specific awareness with my project. I would be happy if it managed to bring back emotions of a lost time. Something existed, but it's not here anymore.

So what are we really talking about here? Is it history, is it the past, is it time? It is obviously not the past itself, but maybe a feeling for the past, a sense of time. I'm trying to open a window through which we can see things and lives that came before us, so that we can discover traces of the past. I'm offering a new framework for experience that stimulates an emotional awareness of the history of the place. And since there are practically no historical traces left, it needed an intense architectural effort to stimulate a feeling for the specific time of the place. So yes, you could say that there is a theatrical aspect to this effort.

ML   So you're staging the landscape?

PZ   Yes, staging and orchestrating it. The museum is a dark box for viewers to look at those few remaining artifacts of the history of the mine that we managed to find. Daylight enters the dark space and falls on the ledges where the objects are displayed. It comes from above, but you cannot see where it comes from, and you cannot look out. Then, at the end of the narrow space, there is a spectacular bay window where you actually do look out. So the short "scenic walk" inside the black box starts with the dim light of the artifacts and ends with this dramatic "lookout" window. You feel completely exposed, standing in a dangerous position above the canyon, where you suddenly see the real thing: the walls of the canyon, precipitous cliffs, the rock faces, and the bottom of the valley, into which the ore was thrown down. I want to evoke emotions powerful enough to get visitors out of their usual mode of passive perception, to rouse them and hopefully acquire a deeper understanding of the place. Yes, I'm dramatizing and I know full well how fine the line is between drama and melodrama.

Anyway, working on this kind of blackness and darkness with the light coming through reminds me of Nabokov once again, who pondered that "common sense tells us that our existence is but a brief crack of light between two eternities of darkness." Where I am it is light, and before me and after me all is darkness, he says. Perhaps that is how I started—a little light here and there to guide you.

ML   Your two Norwegian projects are very different—at least their starting points are. For the witch memorial in Vardø you had nothing physical to start with on the site; in Sauda you have been dealing with an almost invisible industrial ruin. You've been inventing not out of nothing, but out of only minimal traces.

PZ   True, Sauda has a certain *objet trouvé* character to it, while in Vardø there was nothing left but the

name: Steilneset. The witch trials left no physical traces in the landscape. My knowledge came from documents, historical facts recorded in books and, most importantly, from local narratives and memories. So I marked the place where the victims were burned at the stake. It was about commemorating a phenomenon that has no permanent physical shape, and maybe never had one, and the form I invented emerged in part from collaborating with Louise Bourgeois.

In Vardø, I would like to see books made on the physiognomy and character of the place, on the rocks, the vegetation, the birds. When you go to see the Vardø monument, I think people should be motivated to look at the place more closely and to start to learn. To develop an understanding of the time of a place you have to feel its history and look carefully at its present form. Again, the new building with its unique, extremely long and narrow construction of scaffolding along the seashore makes you see the landscape in a new way—and now you want to understand, to learn more about it.

ML   Looking at your projects, the built and the unbuilt, I find them all different and singular. Yet they share a certain family resemblance, encompassing both similarity and difference, a quality not easily explained by worn concepts such as site-specificity, genius loci, and the like. I believe it has to do with a specific way in which you connect your buildings to the ground. Currently this concern with grounding has emerged in projects ranging widely from Allmannajuvet in the Norwegian fjords to an enormous museum inserted into the urban complexity of Los Angeles.

PZ My buildings are grounded in ways that are not formal. I believe it has to do with something more basic and essential. Mircea Eliade talks about certain personal and sacred places that give us a place on earth, that ground us.[11] I like to think that my buildings are grounded in a similar way, to become a *place,* either sacred or profane, so that they can become part of a *home*—for me, for a few, for many.

   In my Norwegian projects I had to deal with powerful, almost primal landscapes, which showed few traces of human interference. The opposite was the case in Los Angeles. The actual physiognomy of the site of the new building that is to house the collection of the Los Angeles County Museum of Art appears rather complex at first sight; it has no clear identity. What you see are different building types, scattered here, densely grouped there. So first I had to understand the different layers of urbanization from the open fields with the famous La Brea Tar Pits, a national landmark where natural asphalt has seeped up out of the ground for tens of thousand of years, to the first Museum of History, Science and Art, which was replaced in 1965 by the new Los Angeles County Museum of Art, a Lincoln Center-like composition of pavilions designed by William Pereira. Among the heterogeneous building patterns that developed over the years—a very special urban palimpsest on two rectangles of the LA grid—today's museum occupies a large central portion.

ML   In this urban palimpsest, the natural history of the site, with the prehistoric tar pits exemplifying what might be termed geological time or the time of the landscape, seems to play an important part in the way you're grounding this enormous structure, even though grounding in this case also involves letting the building as it were "float" above the ground.

PZ   To begin with, there were aspects of the site that I could not reconcile with my ideas for reestablishing something of the original spirit of the place and creating an important (I think the museum deserves this classification) public building that enters into a dialogue with the city. The original William Pereira building had been buried and effectively destroyed by a postmodern museum extension added in the 1980s;

so what we see today is an incomprehensible and rather chaotic cluster of volumes heavily concentrated in one corner of the museum site. Removing this building and the extension will be an act of liberation that I'm longing to see happen in the near future. The ground around the tar pits will then be open again and my new museum will respect that.

An inner line of circulation parallel to Wilshire Boulevard—a spine for the museum inside the lot—was introduced as a result of the architectural competition of 2004. If I had acted on this concept with my new building, the whole museum would have become an internal event inside that block and would essentially have turned its back on the city. So in our first design phase, a freestanding building evolved as another solitaire in the open field next to the tar pit. It had an organic form reaching out with its petals where it could and staying back where it should. Like a plant, it had neither back nor front. In section it showed two freely swinging horizontal plates hovering above the ground, a floor plate and a roof plate, held up by a series of substantial pillars. We called it the "black flower." There was this dream that the liberated ground surrounding the new building would become a modern version of a desert garden: grassland, chaparral, and some complementary plantings adapted to the local climate.

The way the design looks now, the building has liberated itself from the confines of the lot. It does not maintain any classical geometric relationships of urbanization anymore. Designed to be a landmark, it crosses Wilshire Boulevard and lands on the other side of the street. The organic shape has acquired more linear strength, energetic enough to cross the big boulevard with a certain degree of urban energy. Like the "black flower" of the beginning, it is still an all-around, look-out-look-in building composed of two horizontal plates hovering above the ground. Its horizontality answers the horizontality of Los Angeles and makes the Santa Monica mountains that rise to the north even more evident. The new design can now be read as a big sign written over the LA grid. As a large object in the city, I'm trying to give the building a strong archetypal quality. It should feel elemental in material, construction, and shape. Meanwhile, the idea of a desert garden in which the older time of the site continues to resonate is still alive.

ML   Your early comparison of the LACMA design with a "black flower" makes me think of Nabokov again, who writes about "floating islands of water lilies," and of Marcel Proust, who—in what we could think of as an anachronistic, clairvoyant nod to Nabokov—compared water lilies to butterflies. The

water lilies on the river Vivonne, he wrote, "had come like butterflies to rest their glossy blue-tinged wings on the transparent obliquity of that watery bed." Now it strikes me that Proust's water lily descriptions have some urban implications as well. The "watery bed" becomes "celestial," in Proust's water vision:

"It gave the flowers a soil of a color more precious, more affecting than the color of the flowers themselves; and, whether it sparkled beneath the water lilies in the afternoon in a kaleidoscope of silent, watchful, and mobile contentment, or whether toward evening it filled, like some distant port, with the rose and the reverie of the sunset, ceaselessly changing so as to remain in harmony, around the more fixed colors of the corollas themselves, with all that is most profound, most fleeting, most mysterious—all that is infinite— in the hour, it seemed to have caused them to flower in the middle of the sky itself."[12]

Seeing your 1:10 model of a section of the LACMA at the Venice Biennale in 2016, I was reminded of this Proustian imagery. Surrounded by Christina Kim's colorful textiles hung in protective covers, the museum model highlighted the collection and the storage spaces both concretely and metaphorically, as well as demonstrating how the building will reflect its

total environment of city and sky. You have a
lot of experience designing spaces for artworks and
historical objects, but on a smaller scale and by
concentrating on particular, singular objects. What is
it like to deal with the enormity and diversity of
this collection?

PZ   The new building for the collection of the Los
Angeles County Museum of Art is to have a special
quality, because it should not only speak about
the time of its location, but also about the time of the
many artifacts to which it gives a home. Concerning
the objects the building will house, I started out
by saying that the only thing we can do today is to
look at the objects *now.* We cannot look at what
they were way back in time; and that means giving up
old museum ideas and their encyclopedic ambi-
tions. With so many objects from different cultures and
periods, the collection in this museum can give us
great insight into our relationship to history and time.
Rather than showing the artifacts as illustrations
of a presumed historic development, I want to treat
them as objects of culture, objects of art in their own
right, for all of us to experience. We know how encyclopedic museums are laid out with their timelines
and space lines—period halls from the ancient to
the present, from East to West, and so on—reflecting

Enlightenment-period ideas on how to categorize, order, and look at the world, trying to make sense of it all. We see things differently today, and I think that cataloging the world is good, but not good enough.

I think it is important to enable unbiased and unencumbered encounters with the artworks. As an architect, I have to create an appropriate structure for that, spaces where the artifacts like to be, where they start to speak to us, and where we turn soft and tender and open up to their magic. Contemporary art made for museums is only a very small part of the collection that I have to show. Most of the spaces will accommodate artifacts that I like to call "homeless objects," because they have lost their original context. The house I'm designing for them has an open floor plan. The large, contiguous, side-lit exhibition area opening out onto the landscape meanders around enclosed corpuses. Laid out with curatorial care and restraint, the sequence invites visitors to find their own way. The space unfolds according to principles that are part of its seduction. It also has a lot to do with freedom. And while people are strolling, discovering, finding paths of their own, the building, which is open all around, keeps them constantly in contact with the presence of the city so that they never quite lose their bearings. This combination of circulation and orientation coincides with my idea that art, especially ancient art, should be experienced in the context of contemporary life, both literally and mentally.

ML   The idea of seduction and being able to freely move around while enjoying beauty and knowledge recalls the spirit of the ancient *Mouseion*. In the remnants of Alexandria's Mouseion, its name alluding to Mnemosyne's daughters, we can still find traces of that spirit; we can easily imagine the Muses rambling in delightful gardens. The library and its park-like surroundings reflected heavenly landscapes that were also storage spaces for knowledge and the arts. Back in this partly legendary, partly historical setting, the idea of collecting everything in one space, in one place, in one city, in a center of the world, is still comprehensible in all its grandeur.

Even though the LACMA as an institution is younger, it belongs to a trajectory of nineteenth-century public museums that were all about collecting and ordering the world. Yet you seem to be trying to find ways of promoting the singular amid abundance in a museum concept that comes forth as strongly curatorial.

PZ   The floor plan with its open, meandering areas and closed spaces generates an air of extroverted spaces surrounding introverted core galleries. These form a concrete world with an inner autonomy, like the cella of a Greek temple. These might house very special objects, maybe primary objects in Kubler's sense of the term.

Now I can enjoy being in contact with the actual life of the city of Los Angeles—the landscape, the wide horizon—and if I want to, I can also go for the more contemplative silence of the core galleries. It's a little bit like the way Mircea Eliade sees the profane and the sacred; the layout of the museum lives from the tension between the free flow of the profane and the anchored serenity of the enclosed spaces.

But maybe what gives me the best feeling of all is this chance to create a museum for artifacts, a home for pieces of art with spaces where you can experience the light of the sun in the morning, in the evening, in winter and summer, from the north and from the south, the east and the west. I make contact with the cyclical nature of time, I feel as if I'm part of a larger rhythm, and that has a positive impact on the visitors looking at the artifacts and trying to sense their time.

Looking at my design with the eyes of a curator or exhibition maker, I can see them taking advantage of the constantly changing spatial situations, the open flows and the closed spatial sequences, which will allow them to build up entities, vicinities,

juxtapositions, and so on. But most importantly, I believe that the physical, material presence of the architectural space can help the artifacts to radiate their immanent beauty or reveal a strong presence that speaks of a time long gone. I firmly believe that when the surrounding space is right—like a treasure box for a wonderful piece of jewelry—the exhibited object starts to occupy space and develop a special presence. It is only then that you can feel its aura, and even though it might be a functional object or a historical document, like a drinking cup, a carpet, or a ritual mask, you're starting to look at it as a piece of art. Scientific and academic categories are certainly a fruitful underlying tissue of knowledge that we can explore, but we should start with our direct, emotional encounter with the objects. So rather than leaving artifacts alone in the abstract environment of a black box or a white cube, my idea was to stimulate almost physical reactions between two bodies: the architecture and the artifact. That's why the physical presence of the building is so important to me. It provokes an emotional experience, emotional learning.

ML   For all their incomparable differences, both projects, in Sauda and in Los Angeles, hinge on this nonreligious sacredness that seems to have a lot to do with light.

PZ   Of course, space, material, and light—
that's architecture, that's a classic. When designing,
it is easier for me to think about a space as dark,
completely pitch-black, and then allow the light
to come in. The light hits the material, and the material
becomes beautiful. Light hitting surfaces—it's magic.
Shape and form are much more flexible; I change
them all the time to orchestrate the sound of materials,
the chemistry of the real materials, and the right
amount of shadow and light.

At Allmannajuvet there is this communication
between the profane—the road, the parking lot, the
service station—and the "sacred" and enclosed areas.
The pavilions invite people to walk along the old
mining trail, and the first thing they see is the mining
café. The first profane step, if you will, is the invitation
to visitors to have a cup of coffee or some soup.
From there they see the next building clinging to
the cliff across the slope—that is the mining gallery.
And at the very end, half a kilometer further up
the trail, there's finally the mine, its lower entrance
a shockingly small hole in the mountain.

ML   Yet neither mines nor museums are sacred
spaces, even if the nineteenth century proudly
promoted museums as temples of art—a metaphor that
contemporary blockbuster exhibitions love to trumpet.

Whichever way we look at it though, museums are depositories of art, subject to shifting ideals. Mines, on the other hand, were, and still are, profane, not to say dangerous, even lethal places.

PZ   Following Eliade, sacred spaces are places loaded with a sense of spirituality or value—for some-body. They mark a home in the big expanse of space surrounding us. Such a place could be somewhere important from your childhood or somewhere you went with your first love. And you don't have to be religious to feel that such a place is charged with special emotional significance. Earlier in life I used to say that what I'm looking for is a way to create the right atmosphere. But now, talking about the time of my places, I think I'm trying to achieve something that I would call "emotional reconstruction," by which I mean the formal and material qualities my buildings should have when they speak about the time of their place. This, of course, has nothing to do with scientific reconstruction as we know it.

ML   It's refreshing to hear you rethinking the idea of atmosphere. As I've mentioned to you before—also in writing—we've become reluctant to present undergraduates with your writings on atmosphere, because they tend to make them uncritical, vague, and poetic. Then, of course, there is a whole industry of musings on "atmosphere" in contemporary architectural theory. I realize that the reason I'm not particularly attracted to the yoking of atmosphere and architecture is precisely because of its lack of historical impetus; it is simply too cute, and too private. Better then, perhaps, to seek refuge in Nabokov's "Speak, Memory" figure, which has not yet been exploited in architectural discourse. To me, emotional reconstruction promises to be the stronger concept in the endeavor to understand architecture's relationship to history and time.

PZ   There is a complex psychology involved in the relationship of place, building, and function in the eyes of their users. Being in the world, when we use a building we are always stirred by myriad emotions, images, and memories. I like to understand and orchestrate this in my designs. My buildings should feel deep.

We architects often talk about intervention whenever we place a new building on a site; but I'm not sure I like that word too much, because it has an air of superior action. When I speak of emotional reconstruction, what I mean is enabling and stimulating feelings of empathy, maybe even compassion, but also playful curiosity in experiencing a place.

The black volumes and the inner spaces I created for the Sauda project are an attempt to create an emotional environment that bespeaks the vulnerability of those who worked in the mining industry. Both in Kolumba Art Museum and in Shelter for Roman Archaeological Ruins in Chur, I literally recreated spaces that were reminiscent of lost volumes. The imagination is fired, memory can speak.

ML   To state the obvious: We don't need to read Proust to understand that memories are fluctuating contemporaneity. Nabokov also knew all about that. He even speaks about how his memories are no longer quite his own because he has placed all kinds of mundane objects from his past—mirrors, furniture, chandeliers—throughout his fiction, "in the apartment house of a chapter" or "in the hired room of a paragraph," as he puts it, significantly using architectural terms. It makes him feel as though only a few things are left, and that "many have been squandered." He is, in fact, suggesting that both the objects and the memories could be used only once, and that once he has written about them, they are lost to his art. He even admits that he envies the novelist who has managed to "preserve an actual love letter that he received when he was young within a work of fiction," safely stored among otherwise "spurious lives." But is emotional reconstruction an invocation? Is it you as an architect invoking something, or is it there—accessible and shared, here and now?

PZ   Essential to the notion of emotional reconstruction, as I use the term, is that it has the quality of a shared experience. I can compose a piece of architecture with materials, light, shadow, and sound, and give it a presence most people would be able to associate with something in their personal landscape of emotions. We all come from somewhere; we are all full of highly personal images that are dear to us; we are all full of history. I love to work with that. When I first read Aldo Rossi's illuminating book *Autobiografia scientifica* (A Scientific Autobiography) in the 1980s,[13] it became very clear to me that in order to be authentic I would have to work only with my own images. What is it I want to express when I speak about a feeling of history and a feeling of time, and what architectural language do I use to express this? There is no general answer to that. And for sensing the place? Do I have to read about its geology, biology, history? My answer to these questions is always the finished building: crude timber, tar oil paint, screws and bolts, corrugated metal, black industrial coating—this is the vocabulary I speak with in the Sauda project. And in each place,

I want to speak the architectural language that
belongs to that place and resonates with its time.

ML   "Cultural memory touches on something in man
that is older and more durable than his immediate
presence, something that moves him because in
it he meets his immortal alter ego," as Sibyl Moholy-
Nagy, your teacher at the Pratt Institute in New
York in the 1960s, once said. Or to be more exact, this
is what she wrote in 1961 when discussing some
new designs by Paul Rudolph and other "continuity-
starved" architects, who, stifled by their modernist
training, as she diagnosed it, were having "illicit love
affairs" with history. Her essay, titled "The Future
of the Past," alluded to T. S. Eliot's "Tradition and the
Individual Talent" (1919) and was published two
decades before "The Presence of the Past" was taken
hostage by postmodernism in Venice in 1980.[14]
T. S. Eliot's timeless text on tradition, time, and art
deserves to be quoted at some length, as I believe it
somehow resonates with your way of thinking
about architecture and history. Tradition cannot be
inherited, Eliot says, it can be achieved only
through hard labor:

"It involves, in the first place, the historical sense, which
we may call nearly indispensable to anyone who

would continue to be a poet beyond his twenty-fifth year; and the historical sense involves a perception, not only of the pastness of the past, but of its presence; the historical sense compels a man to write not merely with his own generation in his bones, but with a feeling that the whole of the literature of Europe from Homer and within it the whole of the literature of his own country has a simultaneous existence and composes a simultaneous order. This historical sense, which is a sense of the timeless as well as of the temporal and of the timeless and of the temporal together, is what makes a writer traditional. And it is at the same time what makes a writer most acutely conscious of his place in time, of his contemporaneity." [15]

PZ   Thank you, Mari, for reminding me of Sibyl Moholy-Nagy. When I studied at Pratt in the late 1960s, I remember her complaining in her lectures about modern architects disregarding history, and I got the impression that she knew most of them personally. But still under the sway of my modernistic ideas, I was not ready to listen to what she was saying. Of course, she knew it all. I have come a long way.

Notes

1 Vladimir Nabokov, *Speak, Memory. An Autobiography Revisited*
   (1966), New York: Random House, 1989, p. 139.

2 Stendhal, *Love* (1822/1853), trans. Gilbert and Suzanne Sale,
   London: Penguin Books, 2004, pp. 45–47.

3 Stendhal, *Love*, pp. 284–92.

4 Johann Peter Hebel, *The Treasure Chest* (1811), trans. John Hibberd,
   Harmondsworth: Penguin, 1994, p. 26.

5 Josef Albers, *Interaction of Color* (1963), New Haven, CT:
   Yale University Press, 1971, p. 73.

6 Stendhal, Rome, *Naples et Florence* (1826), in: Stendhal, *Voyages
   en Italie,* Bibliothèque de la Pléiade, Paris: Gallimard, 1973, p. 535.

7 Paul Rudolph, "The Essence of Architecture Is Space" (1969),
   reprinted in idem, *Writings on Architecture,* New Haven,
   CT: Yale School of Architecture, 2009, p. 102.

8 Liv Helene Willumsen, *Steilneset. Memorial to the Victims of
   the Finnmark Withcraft Trials,* trans. Katjana Edwardsen,
   publication to accompany the the exhibition in the Memorial Hall
   in Steilneset, Vardø, Finnmark, 2011.

9 George Kubler, *The Shape of Time: Remarks on the History
   of Things* (1962), New Haven, CT: Yale University Press, 2008, p. 8.

10 Neil MacGregor, *A History of the World in 100 Objects* (2010),
    London: Penguin Books, 2012.

11 Mircea Eliade, *The Sacred and the Profane. The Nature of Religion*
    (1957), trans. Willard R. Trask, San Diego, CA: Harcourt Brace
    Jovanovich, 1987.

12 Marcel Proust, *The Way by Swann's* (1913), vol. 1 of *In Search of
    Lost Time,* trans. Lydia Davis, London: Penguin, 2002, p. 174.

13 Aldo Rossi, *A Scientific Autobiography,* New York: The Institute
    for Architecture and Urban Studies, 1981.

14 Sibyl Moholy-Nagy, "The Future of the Past," *Perspecta 7* (1961),
    pp. 65–76, p. 65.

15 T. S. Eliot, "Tradition and the Individual Talent" (1919), in idem,
    The Sacred Wood. Essays on Poetry and Criticism, London:
    Methuen & Co, 1964, p. 49.

Dimitris Pikionis

Dimitris Pikionis (1887–1968) was a Greek architect, trained as a civil engineer and at the École des Beaux-Arts in Paris, who used mostly concrete and local stone for his buildings in Greece. Looking at his work, I sense his familiarity with the classical modernity of his time but also his origins in which his creations are grounded. For the paved paths on the Acropolis he used stone which he had collected from the rubble of older buildings all over town. Thus the paths photographed by Hélène Binet have a specific connection with the history of the place. I like to imagine that Dimitris Pikionis himself lent a hand with the paving of those paths.

Peter Zumthor

Peter Zumthor

works with his Atelier of around thirty people in the alpine setting of Haldenstein, Switzerland, producing architectural originals like the Bregenz Art Museum, Therme Vals, Kolumba Art Museum in Cologne, or the Steilneset Memorial in Vardø.

Mari Lending

is professor of architectural history at the Oslo School of Architecture and Design. Her latest book is *Plaster Monuments. Architecture and the Power of Reproduction* (Princeton University Press, 2017).

Hélène Binet

is an architectural and landscape photographer based in London. She collaborates with eminent contemporary architects, such as Zaha Hadid Architects, Daniel Libeskind, and Peter Zumthor. Her monograph *Composing Space* was published in 2012 (Phaidon).

The text is based on several conversations between Peter Zumthor and Mari Lending that took place from September 2014 to August 2017 on different occasions.

Acknowledgments
Peter Zumthor and Mari Lending would like to thank Monique Zumbrunn for her meticulous supervision of this book project. Hélène Binet would like to warmly thank Dirk Lellau for the careful editing of her photographs.

Photo essay: Hélène Binet, "Collection," 1989, a photographic essay on the "Landscape of the Athens Acropolis" by Dimitris Pikionis
Copy editing: Bronwen Saunders, Basel
Proofreading: Charlotte Eckler, Grafton, MA
Design: Sarah Winter, Hamburg
Image editing: Dirk Lellau, Cologne
Lithography, printing, and binding: DZA Druckerei zu Altenburg GmbH, Thuringia

© 2018 Verlag Scheidegger & Spiess AG, Zurich

© for the texts: the authors
© for the images: Hélène Binet, London

Verlag Scheidegger & Spiess
Niederdorfstrasse 54
8001 Zurich
Switzerland
www.scheidegger-spiess.ch

Scheidegger & Spiess is being supported by the Federal Office of Culture with a general subsidy for the years 2016–2020.

English edition
ISBN 978-3-85881-805-8

German edition
ISBN 978-3-85881-558-3

French edition
ISBN 978-3-85881-812-6